DANGER

USE GREAT CAUTION WHEN
ENTERING INFORMATION INTO
THIS BOOK. AND GUARD IT
WITH YOUR LIFE.

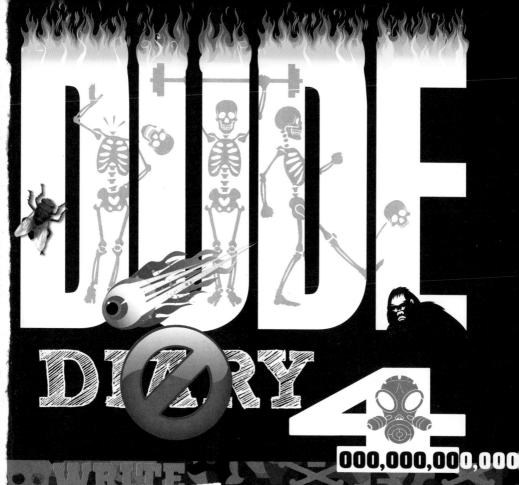

FLY! OR DIE

DUDE DIARY 4

WRITTEN & DESIGNED BY

MICKEY & CHERYL GILL

WHILE BEING HELD PRISONERS ON A BASE ON THE DARK SIDE OF THE MOON UNTIL THEY FINISHED.

FINE print
PUBLISHING

Fine Print Publishing Company
P.O. Box 916401
Longwood, Florida 32791-6401

ISBN 978-189295165-6

2 3 5 7 9 10 8 6 4 1

thedudebook.com

THROW DOWN ALL OF YOUR ACTIVITY ONTO THE FOLLOWING PAGES. THEN LOCK IT UP — BECAUSE SOMETHING THIS PRECIOUS CANNOT BE SHARED WITH MERE MORTALS.

MIX UP MUTANT ENERGY BARS IN A SCIENCE LAB, SHOW AN ALIEN AROUND TOWN, RULE THE WORLD AND DECLARE YOUR OWN HOLIDAY WHILE GETTING READY FOR A GLOBAL GIANT GOLDFISH INVASION.

PREPARE YOURSELF BEFORE TURNING THE PAGE. YOUR PURE GENIUS MAY BE TOO MUCH FOR EVEN YOU TO CONTROL.

GOOD LUCK MY FRIEND. GOOD LUCK.

DUDE DIARY 4

NAME? Ben

LUCKY #? 15

THINK YOU'RE FUNNY?
- ☐ OF COURSE
- ☑ SOMETIMES
- ☐ NOT REALLY

- ☐ JELLY -
- ☑ CREAM -
   FILLED DONUTS?

CAN YOU CURL YOUR TONGUE? ☑ YEP ☐ NOPE

CAN YOU NAME THE CAPITAL OF EACH STATE?
☑ NAH ☐ YEAH

HOW MUCH MONEY DO YOU HAVE RIGHT NOW?

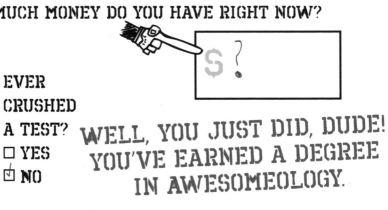

$?

EVER
CRUSHED
A TEST?
- ☐ YES
- ☑ NO

WELL, YOU JUST DID, DUDE!
YOU'VE EARNED A DEGREE
IN AWESOMEOLOGY.

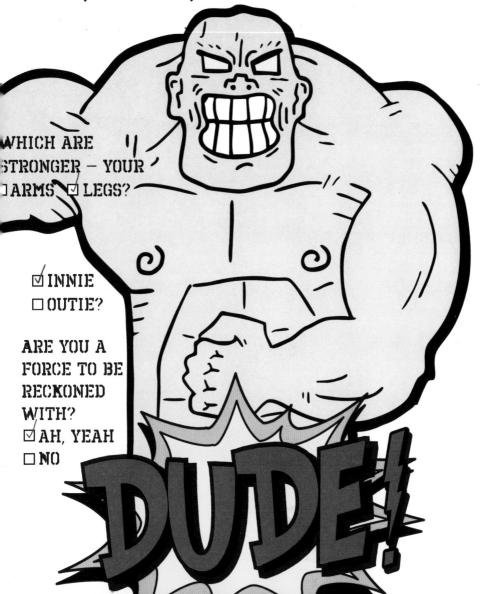

WHICH ARE
STRONGER – YOUR
☐ARMS ☑LEGS?

☑INNIE
☐OUTIE?

ARE YOU A
FORCE TO BE
RECKONED
WITH?
☑AH, YEAH
☐NO

DUDE!

TAKE
CHARG
OF ALL DUDEKIND!

You're boss of the world.
What should all bros do and not do?

DUDE DO'S

DUDE DON'TS

Get it? Dude do.

A GIANT

IS TERRORIZING YOUR TOWN AND **HEADED** TO YOUR STREET!

GOLDFISH

BEFORE U RUN SCREAMING, WHAT WOULD U GRAB FROM YOUR HOUSE?

I would grab my sword that is encrusted with diamonds.

OWN ANYTHING YOU'D TRADE
FOR SOMETHING ELSE?

STUFF YOU'D GIVE UP

STUFF YOU'D LIKE TO GET

Trade _____ for _____

Trade _____ for _____

Trade _____ for _____

Trade _____ for _____

Trade _____ for _____

Trade _____ for _____

Trade _____ for _____

Trade _____ for _____

Trade _____ for _____

WHAT WOULD MAKE AN INSANELY GOOD SUPER BOWL HALFTIME SHOW?

Plan it!

FROM WHERE YOU ARE RIGHT NOW, WHAT CAN YOU . . .

Hear? _____

_____

See? _____

_____

Smell? _____

_____

Taste? _____

I smell myself. I stink!

_____

_____

_____

My Brain.

WHAT WOULD YOU LIKE TO
SUPER

My brother

SIZE?

WHAT
WOULD YOU
LIKE TO
SHRINK?

Famous Person

you would trade places with for 1 day?

What would you do?

IF YOU WERE KING WHAT HOLIDAY WOULD YOU DECLARE?

HOLIDAY NAME

DATE

WHAT WOULD PEOPLE DO ON YOUR HOLIDAY?

WHAT WOULD PEOPLE EAT?

If You answered to
You fill your food

Menu

That's your stomach.

Breakfast

Lunch

Dinner

Snack

Beans & cheese doodles.

AN ALIEN HAS LANDED. HE UNDER-STANDS NOTHING ABOUT OUR PLANET OR HUMANS. WHAT TOP 10 EPIC EARTH THINGS SHOULD HE DO?

OUTER SPACE BRO'S TOP 10

1. _____

2. _____

3. _____

4. _____

5. _____

6. _____

7. _____

8. _____

9. _____

10. _____

1. ☑ Ostrich skateboard derby ☐ C

2. Beverage ☐ with ☑ without a straw?

3. Are your feet dirty? ☐ Yes ☑ No

4. Afraid of spiders? ☑ No ☐ AHHHH! YES! ☐ Yes, but don't tell

5. Ever made a rubber band ball? ☐ Yes ☑ Why would I do that?

6. Good aim with a rubber band? ☑ Excellent ☐ OK

7. How about with spitballs? ☐ Always ☐ Sometimes ☑ Never

8. ☐ Monkey motor cross ☑ Raccoon racecar driving?

9. Scavenger hunts? ☑ Awesome ☐ Annoying

10. ☑ Gorilla basketball ☐ Elephant Ping-Pong?

THINGS YOU CAN DO AT THE SAME TIME

1. _____ & _____

2. _____ & _____

3. _____ & _____

4. _____ & _____

5. _____ & _____

Dude!

CARTOON CHARACTER YOU'D LIKE TO BE FRIENDS WITH? WHY?

CHARACTER NAME

IF YOU HAD YOUR

WAY WHAT KIND OF

CLASSES WOULD YOU

TAKE AT

SCHOOL?

CLASS NAME

WHAT WOULD YOU LEARN ABOUT

What would be incredibly cool to catapult through the air?

CATAPULT

(NOUN)
A MACHINE USED TO HURL AN OBJECT

(VERB)
HURL OR LAUNCH SOMETHING AT GREAT SPEED

HAMBURGER PATTIES!

NAH. COW PATTIES!

A PUMPKIN!

DON'T EVEN THINK ABOUT IT!

ASK OTHER DUDES AND YOUR BROS TOO.

#1

2. _____

3. _____

4. _____

5. _____

6. _____

7. _____

8. _____

9. _____

10. _____

ULTIMAT

WHICH TOTALLY CRUSHES IT?

- SAUSAGE 'N' BISCUIT VS.
- HAM 'N' BISCUIT VS.
- FRIED CHICKEN 'N' BISCUIT

WHY?

_____

_____

_____

_____

- POTATO CHIPS VS.
- CORN CHIPS VS.
- CHOCOLATE CHIPS

WHY?

_____

_____

_____

- YETI VS.
- BIGFOOT VS.
- GRIZZLY BEAR
  WITH A BLACK BELT

WHY?

_____

E CLASH!

Victory is mine.

- STUFFED PIZZA CRUST VS.
- STUFFED FRENCH TOAST VS.
- DOUBLE STUF OREOS

WHY?

_____

_____

- MAGIC WAND VS.
- MAGIC LAMP VS.
- MAGIC CARPET

WHY?

_____

_____

_____

S.

_____

A HUGE COMPANY

NEEDS HELP NAMING ITS NEW

CREEPY CRAYONS.

GIVE 'EM SOME NAMES. THE GROSSER, THE SCARIER, THE WEIRDER THE BETTER.

Melted Greenbeans

Armpit Hair

STICKY

THINGS YOU THINK
R totally awesome?

Gum

Sticky tack

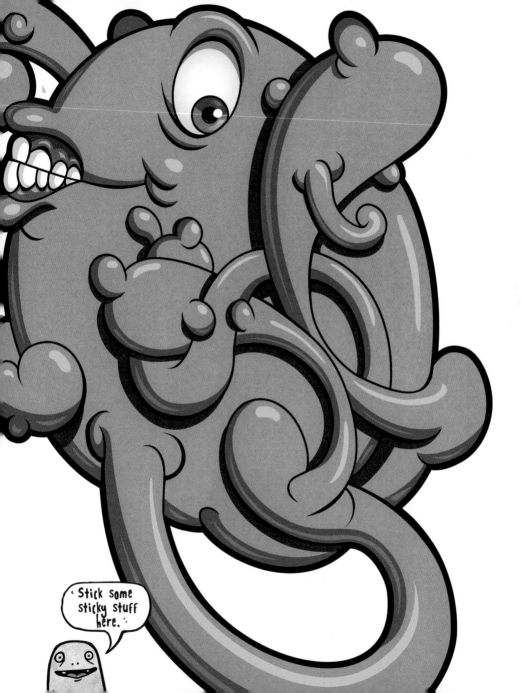

IF YOU WERE A MONSTER
WHAT WOULD YOU BE?

{ Vampire }

WHAT IF YOU WERE A(N)...

CANDY? Hershy Choralate

CAR? Nissan

SMELL? Fart

FRUIT? Kiwi

SHOE? Nike

VIDEO GAME? Madden NFL 12

ANIMAL? Hippiguana

name

**how he/she
describes you**

_____

How would your bros, other dudes, family, teachers, etc. describe YOU?

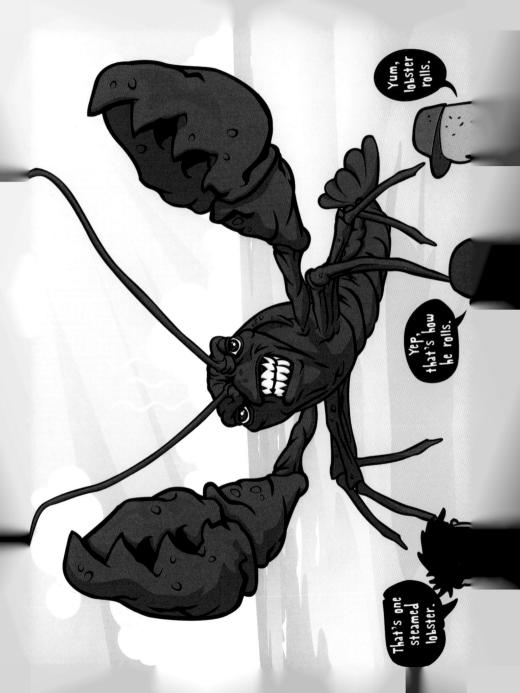

WHAT MAKES YOU

"red hot" mad?

_____

laugh
hysterically?

_____

super sad?

_____

totally
psyched?

_____

beyond bored?

_____

WHAT DO YOU THINK IS OUT THERE BEYOND OUR SOLAR SYSTEM?

_____

_____

_____

_____

_____

_____

_____

1. EVER HIT SOMEONE WITH A S|

2. Can you make a good armpit fart? ☐ Yep ☐ Nope

3. Wash your feet in the shower? ☐ Yeah ☐ Depends ☐ Nah

4. Ever taken a whiff of your earwax? ☐ Yep ☐ Huh? ☐ No, gross

5. Scabs? ☐ Cool ☐ Totally disgusting

6. Do you keep wearing sneakers with a stench? ☐ Yeah ☐ Nah

7. Had a beverage come out your nose? ☐ Yes! ☐ No ☐ How's that work?!

8. Are you a double dipper? ☐ Yes, with pride ☐ Yes, in secret ☐ No way, man

9. Would you consider your gas emissions ☐ lame ☐ fairly foul ☐ deadly?

10. Are your burps ☐ weak ☐ average ☐ a public disturbance?

if you came with instructions what would they be?

AWESOME KID!
COOL BUD!
THE BEST!

THE AMAZING

Name

add your name here

INSTRUCTIONS

1. Feed him _____

_____

2. Let him _____

3. _____

_____

4. _____

_____

5. _____

GIVE HIM FRIES AT LEAST ONCE A DAY.

WARNING

add a warning label

WOULD YOU RATHER GO ON

- A HIGH SEAS ADVENTURE
- AN OUTER SPACE JOURNEY?

Why?

_____

_____

_____

_____

_____

_____

WHY SHOULD SASQU

HE'S GOT AN EPIC NAME
AND A COOL NICKNAME.
MAKE UP YOUR OWN
CRYPTID
AND THEN GIVE HIM AN AWESOME
"BIG" NICKNAME.

_____
Name

_____
Nickname

_____
Where does he live?

_____
What does he eat?

A cryptid is a creature that may or may not exist.

Like Yeti or the Loch Ness monster.

UATCH HAVE ALL THE FUN?

Draw Him

I'm callin' mine BIG MOUTH.

WHAT WOULD YOU LIKE AN UNLIMITED SUPPLY OF?

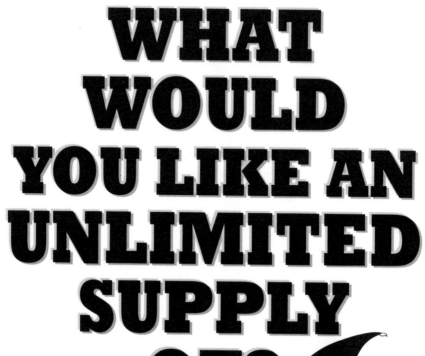

1. _____

2. _____

3. _____

4. _____

5. _____

6. _____

7. _____

8. _____

9. _____

10. _____

WHAT SHOULD IT TASTE LIKE? FLAVORS? INGREDIENTS?

THEY'RE INVENTING VITAMINS AND MINERALS FOR THE BAR TOO. COME UP WITH NEW VITAMIN NAMES AND THE TYPE OF ENERGY OR POWER THEY SHOULD GIVE.

VITAMIN NAME:

ENERGY OR POWER

I was thinking a quadruple chocolate crisp full of vitamin Z29 that would make me invisible in the daylight.

BUILD A TEAM

YOU'RE THE PROUD OWNER OF A

START PLA

SPORT _____

TEAM
NAME **THE** _____

          CITY   MASCOT

TEAM
COLORS _____

TEAM
LOGO

SPORTS
AM

W PROFESSIONAL TEAM IN TOWN

NING, MAN!

DRAW THE UNIFORM

YES!

PULLING MY LITTLE SISTER'S HAIR

FORGETTING TO TAKE THE TRASH OUT

LEAVING THE TOILET SEAT UP

SHOVING DIRTY CLOTHES UNDER MY BED

NOT DOING MY HOMEWORK

THROWING A FOOTBALL IN THE HOUSE

PULLING PRANKS

HIDING MY OLDER SISTER'S LIPSTICKS

BEING TOO LOUD

GETTING IN FIGHTS WITH MY BROTHER

BRINGING LIZARDS INTO THE HOUSE

PUTTING MY HAMSTER IN MY MOM'S BED

NOT LISTENING

WHAT DO YOU USUALLY GET IN TROUBLE FOR?

1 _____

2 _____

3 _____

4 _____

5 _____

Only 5 things?

I'm in trouble 24/7.

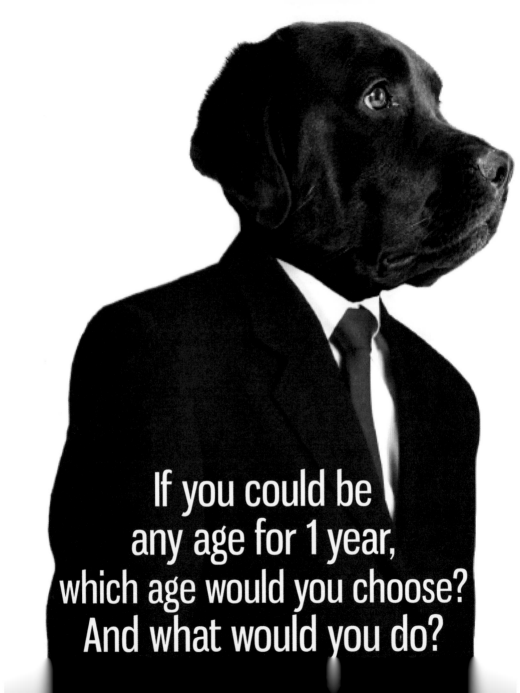

I'd be a 30-year-old prez of a bank for dogs.

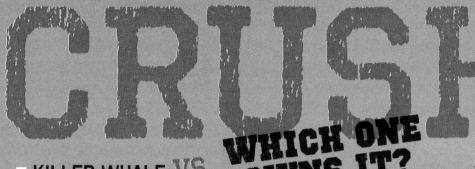

CRUSH

WHICH ONE OWNS IT?

- KILLER WHALE VS.
- KILLER BEES VS.
- KILLER BUNNY

WHY?

_____

_____

_____

- HUMVEE WITH A ROCKET LAUNCHER VS.
- CAMARO TRANSFORMER (BUMBLEBEE) VS.
- BATMOBILE WITH THAT OIL SLICK SPRAYER THINGY

WHY?

_____

_____

_____

_____

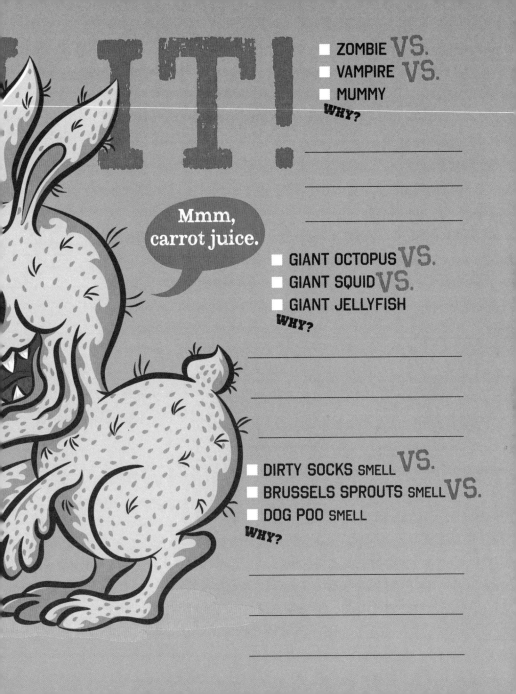

IT!

■ ZOMBIE **VS.**
■ VAMPIRE **VS.**
■ MUMMY
WHY?

_____
_____
_____

Mmm, carrot juice.

■ GIANT OCTOPUS **VS.**
■ GIANT SQUID **VS.**
■ GIANT JELLYFISH
WHY?

_____
_____
_____

■ DIRTY SOCKS SMELL **VS.**
■ BRUSSELS SPROUTS SMELL **VS.**
■ DOG POO SMELL
WHY?

_____
_____
_____

1. WHiCH WOULD Be MOST aMaZiNG?
☐ DOG CROSSED WiTH a DOLPHiN
☐ Cat CROSSED WiTH a HORSE
☐ GeRBiL CROSSED WiTH aN iGuaNA

2. WHat's SCaRY COOLest? ☐ SCORPiON tail ☐ WaSP StiNGeR ☐ TaRaNtuLa FaNGS

3. WHiCH is GROSSeR? ☐ AN eaRWaX MuSeuM ☐ A FaRt SauNa

4. WOULD YOU RatHeR Give UP WaSHiNG YOUR ☐ FaCe ☐ HaiR ☐ Feet?

5. WHat's MORE teRRiFYiNG? ☐ LaNDiNG a Jet ON aN aiRCRaFt CaRRieR
☐ DRiViNG a SeMi tRUCK ON aN iCY ROaD

6. ☐ CaptaiN AMERiCa ☐ THe HULK ☐ THOR ☐ IRON MaN?

7. WHat WOULD Be FUNNieR? ☐ ZOMBie FOOtBaLL ☐ BiGFOOt BaLLet?

8. WOULD YOU RatHeR Be tHe
☐ PRez ☐ ViCe-PRez OF tHe U.S.A.?

9. ☐ PePPeRONi SauSaGe HaM
MeatBaLL Pizza
☐ CHOCOLate PeaNut ButteR
MaRSHMaLLOW CaRaMeL BaRS?

10. WOULD YOU WaNt a ☐ HOt tUB iN
☐ DeLUXe GaMiNG StatiON FOR
☐ SeCRet tuNNeL UNDER YOUR BeDROOM?

□ Ger-Guana? □ Iguerbil?

BE WEREWOLF!

CREATE MORE "WERE" CREATURES

COME UP WITH YOUR OWN OR CHOOSE SOME OF THESE.

TURTLE	LIZARD	COW
CAT	RABBIT	POSSUM
PTERODACTYL	BASS	WALRUS
RAT	TURKEY	OSTRICH

WERE _____

WERE _____

WERE _____

WERE _____

WERE _____

WERE _____

HOLLYWOOD

WANTS YOU AND YOUR FRIENDS TO STAR IN YOUR OWN MOVIE!

WHAT SHOULD IT BE ABOUT?

WHAT WOULD YOU
AND YOUR BUDS
DO IN IT?

SKATEBOARDING OVER A HUMONGOUS HOAGIE!
GIVE YOUR MOVIE A NAME.
ACTION!
Can somebody get Whiskers off the set!
It should for sure be in 3D!
Ugh, I smashed my board.

IF AN X-RAY MACHINE
COULD TAKE A
PICTURE
OF WHAT YOU
THINK ABOUT
A LOT,
WHAT
WOULD
SHOW
UP?

YOUR THOUGHTS

HOW ABOUT YOUR FRIENDS AND FAMILY?

NAME	NOGGIN STUFF

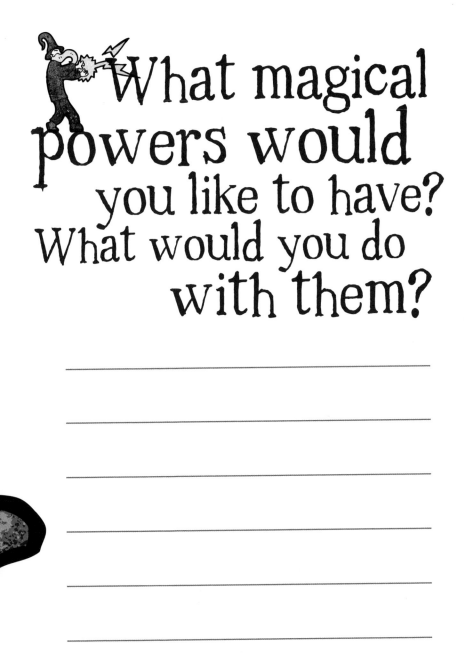

What magical powers would you like to have? What would you do with them?

_____

_____

_____

_____

_____

SAY HEY TO

Give him a cool name.

HE IS AN INCREDIBLY SMART & TALENTED DOG...
AND HE NOW BELONGS TO YOU.

WHAT SHOULD YOU DO TOGETHER?

_____

_____

_____

_____

_____

_____

He could be our new second baseman.

Could he eat my homework for real?

FREAKY FEARS & PHOBIAS

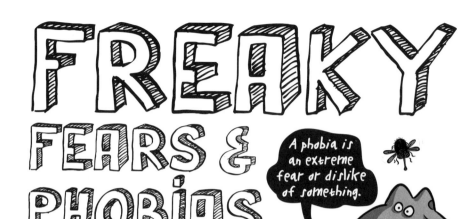

A phobia is an extreme fear or dislike of something.

Ablutophobia – Fear of washing or bathing
Alektorophobia – Fear of chickens
Bogyphobia – Fear of the bogeyman
Consecotaleophobia – Fear of chopsticks
Hippopotomonstrosesquippedaliophobia – Fear of long words

Be afraid. Be very afraid.

Linonophobia – Fear of strings
Lutraphobia – Fear of otters
Myxophobia – Fear of slime
Nephophobia – Fear of clouds
Numerophobia – Fear of numbers
Phronemophobia – Fear of thinking
Pteronophobia – Fear of being tickled by feathers
Pupaphobia – Fear of puppets
Sciophobia – Fear of shadows
Xanthophobia – Fear of the color yellow
Zemmiphobia – Fear of the great mole rat

You should look up the mole rat.

WHAT WEIRD THINGS ARE YOU AFRAID OF?
WHAT ARE YOUR FRIENDS AFRAID OF?
GIVE YOUR CRAZY FEARS AWESOME PHOBIA NAMES.

Scared of lil ole me?

FEARS

PHOBIA NAMES

Frog jumping on my face _____ Frogfaceaphobia _____

_____ _____

_____ _____

_____ _____

_____ _____

_____ _____

_____ _____

_____ _____

 WHERE DO YOU WANNA GO? _____

_____

 WHO SHOULD GO WITH YOU?

_____

_____

 WHAT KIND OF FOOD ARE YOU PACKING?

_____

_____

 WHAT WILL YOU DO FOR FOREST RECREATION?

_____

_____

_____

WHAT KIND OF CLOSE-ENCOUNTER-WITH-A-DANGEROUSLY-WILD-ANIMAL-BUT-YOU-LIVE-TO-TELL-EXPERIENCE WOULD U LOVE TO HAVE? _____

_____

_____

 Not cool. Bigfoot stole our TP!

IF YOU ARE WHAT YOU EAT WHAT WOULD YOU BE?

DRAW YOURSELF OR SCRIBBLE WHAT YOU LOVE TO FEED YOUR GUT.

WHO HAS IT EASIER?

Dudes

OR

Girls

WHY?

SUPERHERO NAME

HOW DID YOU BECOME ONE?

_____

_____

_____

SUPERHUMAN POWERS? ☐ NO ☐ YES, _____

_____

ANY COOL GADGETS? ☐ NO ☐ YES, _____

_____

_____

_____

SIDEKICK? ☐ NO ☐ YES, _____

_____

WHAT...

is the coolest trick
or stunt you can do? _____

are you always being
told to **STOP** doing? _____

do you think happens to
socks lost in the wash? _____

is your favorite word to say? _____

do you think makes
the Internet work? _____

is your gamertag? _____

new electronic device
do you **THINK** u need? _____

is the stinkiest
thing you own? _____

was the last thing
you barfed up? _____

do you think happens to everything
in the toilet after you flush? _____

WRITE or DRAW

all the stuff you can't stand doing that you pretty much have to do, then DESTROY!

Get ink all over it, drop paint on it, staple it, rip it, drag it through the mud.

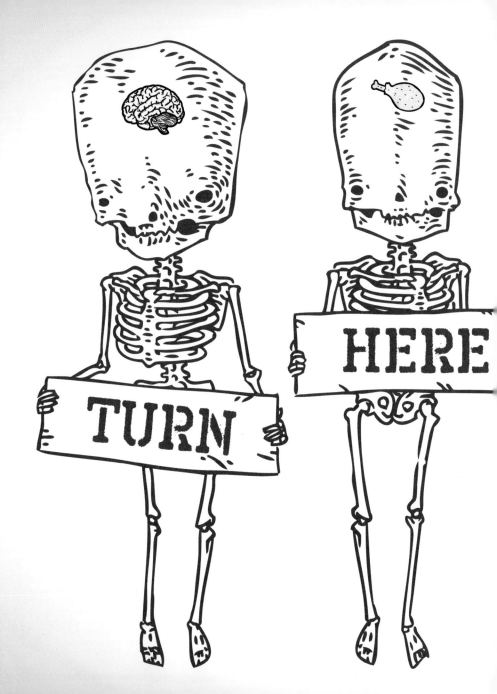

TO COUGH UP ALL OF YOUR BRO-RIGINAL IDEAS

SCRATCH, SCRIBBLE, AND **CLAW** YOUR WAY THROUGH THESE PAGES. OR, JUST KEEP YOUR **GUM** THERE UNTIL YOU WANT TO CHEW IT AGAIN.

IF YOU DARE!

DUDE, you're scary good.

WRITE, DRAW, DESTROY...

IF YOU DARE!

WRITE, DRAW, DESTROY...

WE'RE GETTIN' KILLED IN THIS GAME!

IF YOU DARE!

DUDE, WE'RE ALREADY DEAD!

WRITE, DRAW, DESTROY...

IF YOU DARE!

WRITE, DRAW, DESTROY ...

i have no idea what to write.

IF YOU DARE!

it's because you don't have a brain!

IF YOU DARE!

WRITE, DRAW, DESTROY ...

Dude, you'll wake the dead!

IF YOU DARE!

WRITE, DRAW, DESTROY...

IF YOU DARE!

WRITE, DRAW, DESTROY...

Oh yeah.

IF YOU DARE!

WRITE, DRAW, DESTROY...

IF YOU DARE!

WRITE, DRAW, DESTROY...

i've lost my head!

IF YOU DARE!

 WRITE, DRAW, DESTROY...

IF YOU DARE!

WRITE, DRAW... DESTROY...

IF YOU DARE!

Hey bag of, bag of bag of, bag of bones, swing!

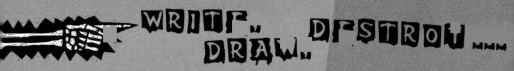

WRITE.
DRAW.
DESTROY...

IF YOU DARE!

WRITE, DRAW, DESTROY ... IF YOU DARE!

DEAD END

SO, YOU MADE IT
THROUGH ALIVE.
WELL DONE EARTH
CREATURE. YOU MUS
NOW GIVE THE GREY
MATTER BETWEEN
YOUR EARS SOME MU
NEEDED DOWNTIME
BEFORE ENGAGING I
EVERYDAY ACTIVITI
WITH YOUR FELLOW
HUMAN RACE.